The Very Small Mammoths of Wrangel Island

by Craig Finlay

Crossroads Poetry Series
Three Fires Confederacy
Waawiiyaatanong ✦ Windsor, ON

First Edition: February 2021

Library and Archives Canada Cataloguing in Publication

Title: The very small mammoths of Wrangel Island / by Craig Finlay.

Names: Finlay, Craig, 1981- author.

Description: First edition. | Poems.

Identifiers: Canadiana (print) 20200252496
          Canadiana (ebook) 20200252526
          ISBN 9781988214375 (paperback)
          ISBN 9781988214382 (PDF)

Classification: LCC PS3606.I53 V47 2020 | DDC 813/.6—dc23

Book cover design: D.A. Lockhart
Cover Image: "Wooley Mammoth" by William Hartman
Book layout: D.A. Lockhart
Author Photo: Carmin Vance

Published in the United States of America and Canada by

 Urban Farmhouse Press
www.urbanfarmhousepress.ca

The Crossroads Poetry Series is a line of books that showcases established and emerging poetic voices from across North America. The books in this series represent what the editors at UFP believe to be some of the strongest voices in both American and Canadian poetics.

Printed in Chaparral Pro

for Nicole

Contents

I

Nothing much happened during the thirty thousand years between the appearance of modern humans and the agricultural revolution. And I think there must have been several someones in that span who lived long full lives and were missed, or mastered a craft or devoted themselves to art. It worries me that I've already forgotten so much about college, let alone high school. I should start storytelling. Telling to remember. The firelight as I dance and sing songs of Homecomings past, of the time I watched Jeremiah get a hand job under the bleachers. Create a new oral tradition. Leave behind strange etchings on hip bones and cave walls, the meaning of which will elude academic consensus.

The universal constant is to end up in orbit. We get trapped in them. Galaxies orbit galaxies and stars the black holes at their centers and planets the stars and moons some of the planets and me a little town in Western Illinois not too far from the Bernadotte dam where I once spent the afternoon reading the *Spoon River Anthology*. I was young and sad and liked that sort of performance. When I finished I felt poetic and sealed the book in a Ziploc and tossed it into the churn where drunk men sometimes fell into the water and did not surface again for months if they surfaced again at all. Sometimes they would get fished out of the water downriver at Havana. Water. That's another constant. The amount of water on earth has remained the same for four billion years, from river to lake to snow to blood and back again. I smoked and waited for the bag to resurface and wondered whether the same water molecules ever returned. If, having traveled from river to river all the way down to the Gulf of Mexico, up the Gulf Stream, then maybe skyward into a nor'easter and inland along storm fronts, they finally completed their orbits along these same muddied banks. And how many times they'd managed the trip since Edgar Lee Masters wrote *The Hill*.

A polar bear's liver is poisonous. One single gram contains enough vitamin A to cause signs of toxicity in humans. Native hunters knew this and were wary of the liver. In 1841 four British sailors became stranded on Stefansson Island while trying to find the Northwest Passage. They killed a polar bear and her cubs for food. Three of them, already exhausted and half-starved, died from Vitamin A poisoning. As the mother polar bear lay bleeding out on the ice, watching the tiny figures approach her and her cubs, she let out a cough, a half-laugh, a fine spray of blood across the pack ice as she called out to them: Enjoy the meal, you fuckers. Especially the liver.

The first permanent colonial settlers of what is now North America were three male slaves who ran away from a Spanish settlement in what is now South Carolina and were forever free after the Spanish could no longer stand the malaria and sailed back home. The Spanish used the word *cimarrón* to refer to slaves who escaped to go live with the Natives. *Cimarrón* was also the name of their cattle. It is the origin of the English word "maroon." As in, to be marooned on an alien planet. I wonder if any of them married. If lovers sang them sweet, sad things by the flicker of low firelight. If they felt like they'd been marooned or if they felt like explorers and stared into distances just soaked with mystery.

Mariners didn't figure out how to calculate longitude until the 18th century. Latitude is easy; just look for the North Star and measure the angle. But longitude? The whole rotation of the Earth thing made that kind of measurement impossible. Sailors died because of this. Crossing the Atlantic from East to West and back and not knowing how far they'd gone. At Scilly in 1707, 2,000 men drowned for want of longitude. The solution was the Marine Chronometer. A clock that could work at sea without the waves throwing off the pendulum. Compare the time on the clock with sunrise and you know your time zone, know how far you are from shore. That saved lives. The first travelers to obsess about the time back home.

How to get your son to go to business school if you catch him experimenting with the humanities: On his 13th birthday tell him that when they finally deciphered cuneiform they found that most of the clay tablets are receipts for livestock. The Sumerians were pushing weight and realized they couldn't trust each other to remember what they bought from whom and for how much so they invented the receipt. And for years everyone wondered what secrets they contained, these thousands of tablets, discarded in the sand. They were discarded because after a while you no longer have to prove that you bought a herd of goats from Taribatum of Ur.

The most famous photo of the Loch Ness Monster was apparently just a plastic dinosaur head attached to a toy submarine. You know the one. The black, curved neck of the thing arcing up and back out of the water. The diagram I saw was quite convincing. I don't understand why people spend so much time and effort proving that the Loch Ness Monster isn't real. Or how crop circles were really made with a board and two ropes. Or that the Phoenix UFOs are really flares fired from fighter planes. They're not helping anything. One time I buried a charcoal briquette for two days, expecting it to become a diamond. Can you imagine if that had worked? The entire diamond industry would collapse.

November, 2018: An otter has set up shop in a Vancouver park famous for its prized koi fish. So far it has eaten 11 of them and they're desperately trying to catch it because each koi is worth between $1,000 and $5,000. They're evacuating the fish. There is a reason why we all root for Godzilla as he stomps on tanks and punches his way through buildings and laughs off the fighter planes that ineffectually buzz around him. We root for Godzilla because there are things of which we all long to be reminded. Like how an office building is only steel and glass and quite imperma-nent. Or that skylines and streets are not mountains and can-yons. Like the true value of a fish.

Consider who can afford the oyster. The value of a blackout poem as opposed to the book destroyed. The professor of poetry and the favorite, prettiest graduate assistant make their way down quiet highways after the Collapse. She strikes a comely pose, lean of flank and vulnerable on the pavement, framed by abandoned cars. The professor lies in wait with a rifle. Later, they dry long strips of flesh over campfires while they workshop poems. Every death is sincere, and they know they must create art in recompense. They leave behind a trail of poems, wrapped in plastic and weighted down with rocks or else tucked into dry, safe places. Copies upon copies so one dies needlessly. The flesh nourishes only their bellies. Their poetry will someday nourish the world's soul.

My uncle, my mother's brother, tells me about the commercials he likes. He says he likes the Bud Light Beer commercials with the king who locks up people who like other beer. He told me he no longer has the attention span to read books. He once wrote them. He only drinks Diet Coke. We are mostly water and he never drinks it. Homeopaths believe water has memory. That if you soak something in water it will remember the properties of that thing forever, no matter how much you dilute it. I wonder if the North Sea remembered the Titanic's passengers as they thrashed and drowned lay still in cold, calm waters. And if those memories carried themselves along storm fronts to Europe, watering fields in France that would soon see trenches and gas and miseries beyond imagining. And if the trees that drank the rain somehow knew something bad was coming.

Fritz Haber discovered the method for large-scale synthesis of nitrogen fertilizers, a process that now enables production of half the world's food supply. He also pioneered the development of poisonous gas in warfare, specifically chlorine gas but also a few other, less famous, ones. He developed "Haber's Rule," a simple calculation. The rule states that small amount of gas over a long period of time will kill someone just as well as a large amount of gas over a short period of time. His wife killed herself over this. He remarried. Won the Nobel Prize. I know someone else would have discovered how to synthesize nitrogen fertilizer. I know someone else would have developed chlorine gas. But don't think for a moment that makes any of this okay. Any of it.

After the Battle of Waterloo soldiers scavenged teeth from the dead for the rapidly growing market for dentures. The oldest dentures date back to the Etruscans but they never really caught on in Europe until the 19th century. You could sell your teeth back then, if you were desperate enough. The wealthy chewed fine steaks with the teeth of the poor. You can still sell yourself, of course. I see the desperate people lining up to sell their plasma for 50 dollars at Octapharma. That's different though. Plasma replenishes. Teeth don't. We only sell ourselves sustainably now.

I watched a cat walk the length of the Stone of the Pregnant Woman at Baalbeck. The stone is immense in a way that makes you think of how fleeting even a nation can be. It was so large they couldn't move it after it was quarried. Sixteen hundred tons. The cat paced at the end, the exact spot where eleven centuries ago a girl named Zaina sat, feet-a-dangle, watching the lamp lights come up one by one in the valley. She smirked and rubbed her belly. The air was thick with hyacinth then. Oils. Long after the world was Rome. Eleven centuries later the woman I'd convinced to come with me to tour Baalbeck was cold and unexpectedly religious and eager to leave. She took a taxi back to Beirut and I stuck around to explore the town alone. I bought a pint of arak at a cornershop and started drinking. The cat watched as I climbed the stone in my worn-out Chuck Taylors and rubbed against my side as I smoked and drummed my feet against this thing archaeologists are still arguing about. How it was meant to be moved. Rolled, or pulled. Something about water. The cat was black and heavy with milk. I tried to feel mysterious but gave up quickly. I don't think men can understand much in the way of mysteries.

There was a city in what is now Eastern Turkey called Ani. It was known as the City of 1001 Churches and those churches shepherded 100,000 souls. If you look now — a single cathedral in a grassy plain, scatterings of walls and stone. Something out of Byron or Shelley. Ani was conquered an unusual number of times. By the mid-17th century the population consisted of five monks living in a ruined monastery. One day they left. Dry grass crunched beneath their feet, kindling for the next wildfire. They carried a young crippled brother and took turns on the task. He watched the towers and rooftops pass through his sight. They forded the river into Armenia and the banks were thick with and thorny vines that tore their robes. They passed an abandoned pup, its eyes not yet open. It nosed the air and whimpered. As Brother Armin brought a rock down on its head a ten-thousand strong bird flock of starlings took to the skies around the city and spelled the true name of God several hundred years too late to have any effect on the course of human history. The brothers walked on and passed the time singing songs of things they already did not know to be truth or legend.

The courtyard of the House of Wisdom by moonlight. The air pregnant with lamp oil and jasmine flowers. Stars seem to crash into Baghdad rather than rise. A literal starfall. They come in waves. Muhammad ibn Musa al-Khwarizmi watches them through the lamp smoke. Outside, somewhere in the fractal streets, someone plays an oud and sings of a lost lover. Ordinarily, al-Khwarizmi would know that this is all of God. The jasmine, the stars, the music. What else but God the pain of an absent lover, the chords on strings? Often on the roof the geometric tile patterns in moonlight send him into seizing ecstasy. Tonight, though, he is fractured. Earlier, he watched a grim little goblin of a man beat a pony to death with a club for its refusal to move. And al-Khwarizmi did not shake that image in the House, or its library, or the baths. There are places where the world is yet broken into parts, he said to his assistant, who brought him mint tea in the moonlit courtyard. Broken and but for any ways my love might be flawed I would bring them back into reunion.

One of the few people conclusively proven to have The Sight was a tiny blind boy who lived in Karnak when it was yet young. He listened to the warbling, cough-like call of the egrets in the water. A scribe named Amenemope found him and saw that he had The Sight and brought him sweet dates and wrote down the secrets the boy learned from Bennu in its egret form. He did not record the boy's name. The boy told Amenemope that he knew the scribe would write the secrets as his own but that did not matter because they belonged to no one. He told Amenemope that some other people would take the secrets in turn and place them in a great book and pass them off as their own but Amenemope didn't believe him. Egrets couldn't always be trusted, after all. Nor did he believe that, 27 centuries hence, grave robbers would steal the scribe's body. That they would sell it and it would make its way north where people would eat parts of it as medicine. Or that they would grind up the rest of it to make paint. All of these things happened. Today you can see little bits of Amenemope in bark of the fallen tree beside the stream in John Everett Millais' *Ophelia*. His heart is safe, though, just as the boy promised. The men did not find it. It weighs just slightly more than a feather.

The last woolly mammoth died 3,600 years ago. The Great Pyramid of Giza was already a thousand years old and there were still mammoths. All of the other mammoths died out during the last Ice Age but a tiny colony survived on a small island north of Siberia and due to something called insular dwarfism they became very small. The last ones were only about three feet tall and weighed a couple hundred pounds. They told stories, though. They watched the Aurora Borealis and told their children that once they were giants. Mighty and strong and the earth shook for them. They would gather on hilltops and look south and raise their trunks and call out to the world: We're still here! We're still here! You aren't done with us yet! We are small but we persist!

The oldest known flute is a length of mute swan bone with three holes drilled in it, found in a German cave in 2008 after being discarded about 43,000 years ago. There are etchings on the walls in the same cave. Several carved ivory figures were found as well. A half man, half lion. A figure with its arms thrown skyward in adoration and prayer. The mute swan does not have a lovely call. More of a chirp. It is called the mute swan because it is less vocal than other swan species. The flute made several lovely notes. Before the first crops were planted men were already discovering they could make the world more beautiful with a blade.

And do you remember the story of Picasso's trip to the Chauvet Caves? He saw the walls filled with charcoal drawings of bison, cave lions, hyenas. Hundreds of them, these thunderous and fierce things that once claimed dominion over the wild places of Europe. Leaving, he either exclaimed, "We have invented nothing," or "After Chauvet, all is decadence." Either could function as an end to a poem about art, if taking in very different directions. Sadly, he said neither. The stories are apocryphal. Chauvet wasn't discovered until 20 years after Picasso died.

Recently, Spanish archaeologists discovered that Neanderthals created art as well. It was long assumed that they created no art and were at best imitators of Cro Magnon crafting. Yet here was art, art that waited sixty thousand years in a Spanish cave. Sixty thousand. Someone put their hand on that cold smooth stone and created a stencil by spitting red pigment over flesh and stone alike. And what if art is natural? This is what worries me. What if it is no better or worse than the flash of obsidian and spray of blood, the dull wet crunch of a club entering a skull, the moon that clings to Nótt's pale breasts as she rides her stallion through the night sky?

Isn't it rather poetic, though, that same fields that saw thousands of men choke to death on Haber's gasses now grow crops nourished by Haber's fertilizers? Isn't it? I think it is. I think it's just the most poetic thing. I'm glad I included it.

II

I'm ready for you to tell me all the ways I hurt you. And by that I mean, I'm ready to sit and really listen. I won't distract you with stories. Like how the word blue doesn't appear anywhere in the Bible. It's also absent from The Iliad and the Odyssey and the Old Testament and some people think this evidence that they didn't have a word for blue. That they couldn't see blue yet because they couldn't manufacture it. That we don't develop words for colors until we can make them ourselves. Maybe they just didn't have the words because they couldn't ever bear to sit and hear about all the pain they drove into lover's hearts. But now? Miles Davis was kind of blue. Gershwin wrote a rhapsody in it. We aren't smarter than the ancients, we just remember them and the stories they left behind as a warning to children listening under the shade of some distant and future tree.

List every self-improvement list, bird feathers and bits of Christmas garland salvaged and re-purposed, packed with mud. I showed up drunk because I felt like singing strange codes to you. The bright things glowed strangely, a shear of light on the ridge line of a different latitude and this was just a bad year. Find the code that cracks you. Every aria, each airplane thick with sight hangs at your heels like your mother's breath, leaving quick little footprints poolside. My own implications are thin and shimmer (the opening of Plainsong). I stay in bed, I finish my coke-scrawled fever dream, until a hole in the wall says the one truest thing, until I unwind myself down the troughs of your hand-me down labyrinth.

He is a boy drowning. Grasping at straws refers to the desperation of a drowning man who grabs onto anything to save himself, even if it cannot possibly help. But drowning doesn't look like drowning. The drowning response draws in the arms and stiffens the legs to preserve energy. Drowning people can't grasp at anything. They can't call for help. A falling, drowning boy will leave a tunnel through the water for his ghost to follow on the way back up. The water may shift it so it looks rather like a root or a lightning bolt but the ghost finds its way by smell, and I've been told it smells strongly of lilacs in summer. They never asked his permission, never even gave him the option to consent. And it is universally agreed that saying no would, at this point, be a terrible and tragic thing. Me? I won't know until I find my way back up, the water growing lighter during the surface, and Ha! How funny you all look treading water, backlit by the sun. I can see why a shark would want a taste of you, slathered in coconut oil and strung out long like a writhing, chaotic buffet.

I want to rename every street on a rotating basis for the most recent pet struck and killed while crossing. There are so many fucking Elm Streets. I want to ask my street who is a good street. You are. Yes you are. Yes you. I want a weekly column in the paper right beside the police blotter announcing which streets are renamed for which dogs and cats complete with pictures. I mostly want my drug dealer to tell me he's moved and I should now stop by his place on Mr. Whiskers avenue.

I am unable to pass by an abandoned toy ball without at least trying to take it home with me. I have pulled them from rivers, I have circled around and driven along with my car door open to grab them from the street, I have carried them out of the woods, I have pulled them down from the branches of trees while walking to work. And I always feel bad because I never end up playing with them very much. I know they must be secretly disappointed in me, even if they're too polite to say anything.

I once thought that I'd live in a boxcar when I was older. Not one I bought and renovated and turned into a home but one still attached to a train. It would trundle from town to town. The chandelier would swing. My parents had multiple chandeliers. Cheap things with dangling imitation crystals. I assumed I would have them too. I still see no reason why a train shouldn't let me live in it.

Millennials are a drowned generation. They live thrashingly. Don't be surprised when the generation you force to start out with debt that hangs on them like a sand dune refuses to buy diamonds or play golf or even patronize casual dining chain restaurants. The Boomers are the worst generation. Who else could pen a desperate plea in Business Insider for everyone to band together and save TGI fucking Fridays?

A few years ago I took to sitting by the train tracks on the way home from work and drinking vodka. I'd pretend I was a hobo and down a half pint of vodka in quick, searing gulps. Vodka so my wife couldn't smell it. Vodka in the trees where no one could see me from the road. Others had used this place. There were liquor bottles and cans of Hurricane High Gravity Lager. I've always loved trains. When I was little I'd pretend to be hobo, too. I had a bundle I'd carry around and my dad took me downtown to watch the freight trains roll through and sometimes one of the cars would be open and I knew that eventually I'd jump into one and go see what the world was like. I saw a photo essay a few years ago, "American Vagabonds," I think it was called. About gutter punks who ride trains around the country. They seemed to drink an awful lot.

I don't really think too deeply on comfort. I just feel like I missed appreciating the part of my life when poverty was proof of living. Not real poverty, of course. More like, art school poverty. Five roommates in a two bedroom apartment in Chicago poverty. Thrift store wardrobes and the thin body to pull it off. Poverty with end. Good discipline. When I see Chicago I want to ask it what I could have done differently, if we ever had a chance. I did drink wine I found on the street in Paris, steal food from a hostel fridge, I did make love to a poet in a park. I used to look up her poems when I was drunk and pretend I was publishing them in my zine in a tiny apartment in Montmarte. Laying out pages and smoking hand-rolls and my one-eared tomcat stretches and yawns on the windowsill. This is a tended garden gone to weeds. Which is okay. I never understood what people have against dandelions.

I never had to wrap the slick, shimmering body of a bluegill in paper towels and bury it with a garden trowel in the back yard. And I didn't need to scrawl a date in marker onto a popsicle stick tombstone. In fact, the fish did not die at all on the way back from Shaw Creek, though it was miles and warm. It learned new ways of breathing as I walked and by the time I passed the public library it was already doing simple tricks and responding to its name.

The ghost of Bob Marley and the ghost of Jacob Marley both came to me on Christmas Eve. The ghost of Bob Marley told me my spirit will walk the earth dragging every vacuum cleaner I ever threw away, their cords tied around my ankles. The ghost of Jacob Marley told me not to worry too much about it. He said ghost chains don't weigh any more than ghosts. Ghost Jacob Marley is really mailing it in at this point. I woke up back in my bed grateful I don't own vacuum. That same morning my friend gave me a Christmas ornament as a present: a plastic tin of sardines. I hadn't even put up a tree.

It's true. I went to a crossroads at midnight. I did not expect to meet the Devil. And I wasn't disappointed. I did meet Jesus Christ though. Really. He was checking his watch and bummed a Parliament from me. I asked him if he was here to meet Lucifer. Yeah, he said. I was just wondering how he's doing, you know? He asked me if I wanted any miracles and I couldn't think of a single thing. I thought of plenty on the way home, though. Isn't that always the way of it? The French call that *L'esprit de l'escalier*, though it refers more to arguments than requests for miracles.

How to convince your child to become a 19th century prison reformer: Take her to Harar, in Ethiopia. The residents feed the hyenas who come into the city at night. Butchers give them leftover beef bones. Some feed them by hand. Outside of the city, the hyenas behave much as we've come to expect. Once on the streets of Harar, though, they're as docile as a shelter dog. Elsewhere in Ethiopia hyenas may attack livestock or even children but not in Harar. Whisper to her, right as their jaws crunch a cow bone and the marrow sprays onto the street: *If you don't feed the people, they'll find a way to feed themselves.*

How to convince your child to become a real estate developer. Take her to Harar. Explain that the symbiotic relationship with the hyenas came about because butchers needed to get rid of their bones and hyenas are the only animal with jaws strong enough to crush them. Mention that tourism has really sprung up as people come to see the hyenas. Whisper in her ear, right as a tourist posts a selfie with a hyena: *The world full of ways to make money. It's almost like it was designed for it.*

How to convince your child to grow up to volunteer at the local co-op. Forego the trip to Harar. Watch the Planet Earth II episode about it instead, including the fucking heartbreaking part where the baby turtles born on the beach get confused by the lights of the city and walk away from the sea instead of toward it. They walk and walk and never find the water. They fall into storm drains. They get smashed by cars and feet. The people do not help them. Some simply push themselves along the pavement until they die. Explain that we've killed 90 percent of big fish over the past century, that neonicotinoid pesticides have killed the same percentage of bees and butterflies. Make it all better by taking her to the co-op and feasting on lentils and sparkling water. Take her to buy a baby turtle from the pet store and name it Lacroix and give it a good, long, life. Stop feeling like writing poetry is just a way to feel better about your own small part in all of this.

Buy a fiddle.

Play.

How to inspire your child to become a spoken word poet, to move to Humboldt Park, to scream into the night and into open mics a call to burn this motherfucker down. Take her to Harar. Show her the butchers feeding the hyenas in the town square. As she watches the feast, explain that we are neither the butcher nor the hyenas. We're the bones. Go home, save up a quarter million dollars. Send her to the Art Institute of Chicago.

III

Millennials are killing serial killing. Over the past 30 years millennial preferences for mass shootings has come at the expense of traditional murder. According to Dr. Mike Aamodt of Radford University, the number of serial killers peaked in 1989 at 193. By the end of the 20th century that number dropped to 107. Currently, it is estimated that there are fewer than 50 active serial killers in the United States. While some of the decline is attributable to improved law enforcement forensic capabilities, many see the decline as indicative of the erosion of the traditional American work ethic. Whereas serial killing requires years of patient effort and highly personalized murder, mass shootings are more in-line with the millennial love for instant gratification. If a serial murder is a personalized letter to a friend, mass shootings are a tweet, a Facebook status, an Instagram post waiting for likes and shares and #thoughtsandprayers.

Everyone should write 100 haiku about the town they left. It doesn't need to be the one they were raised in, just the one they left. I have and it was very instructive. Nikki told me crows brought presents to her mother. Her mother fed them and they started leaving gifts in return. Shiny things, mostly. Soda can tabs and foil from cigarette packs. Things not of crows but of people. I never believed her until she showed me the collection of crow gifts kept in a coffee can on the back deck. Buttons and Christmas tree garland, some coins, a matchbox car. Of course, this wasn't proof, exactly. I never personally saw the crows bring anything, but around haiku 60 or so I noticed I had started writing some wonderfully true things about the genus *corvidae* as they feature quite prominently in my memories of rural Illinois Novembers.

Several times I've written about all those evenings alone on a Beirut rooftop, drinking wine and smoking and watching the lights come up in the mountains. The Doppler effect of mopeds on the streets below and Lebanese TV and Arabic music clear and loud from open windows across the narrow streets beside. I say this as if it were my Sputnik moment, my glimpse the future moment, my we were promised jet packs moment. But it's not a way to tell you I could almost see it. Really, it's a way for me to remember the times I felt the dull distant thud of a needle settling in to the groove in a record exactly the size of the world

If I were to pluck this dead thing from the road then some last bits of breath would escape with a tone more musical than anyone has a right to expect. The echoes of it would roll across the hills like dense fog or a sheep herd. I'll wait for you to experience this wonder with me.

For a while there was a website that let you watch unsecured webcams around the world. Sometimes they were inside people's houses, sometimes cafes or bars. A street food stall in what seemed like Thailand. Open all night and kids hanging out with no thought of curfew. An office in India and the street through the front windows full of mopeds and people. A dark kitchen in someone's home on the other side of the world. Sometimes I could see their ghosts. The ones who come out at night when they think no one is watching. Sometimes a cat. It was so much fun, not because I liked spying on people, but for the same reason that I used to stare at the lit windows in photos of city skylines at night, imagining lives, not thinking that most of them were probably just people working late or custodial staff. When I knew that they must all walk home along slick black pavement and through columns of steam pouring from sidewalk grates. Even now, when I walk home alone I sometimes feel like even the moon could love me.

Day one, drink at least two pints of vodka. Sober for four days and now the pressure is there. I've been lying in bed staring at the wall since I got home. I'd like to pretend it was a fight, but I find myself at Mega Liquor and Smoke on Mishawaka and the clerk knows my brand and how much. The pints are bought singly, along with a couple of one shooters each time. The first pint is intended to be the last pint, but it rarely is. Within the hour cigarettes, drinks on the porch and saying real things to old friends on Facebook chat. Earlier in the day I read a depressing article: 75% of silent films are missing and lost forever. Left to rot or recycled or just thrown away. And now it's too late. We never heard them cry out.

Day two: The hangover will be unbearable. Start drinking at noon if it is Saturday and three if a work day. Of course I'll go too far. Alcohol has diminishing returns the further you go into a bender. End up drinking at least as much as night one, just happy that I feel good. Just trying to make it out of this terrible, awful, no good, very bad day. Today I learned on Reddit that there are only three words in the English language pluralized with "en" instead of an "s" and no one really knows why: ox, child, brother.

Day three: Probably vomiting around 3 a.m. Wake up so thirsty that I was dreaming of drinking decadent amounts of water. Call off work and drink NyQuil and take muscle relaxants to sleep it off. Hopefully sleep until 2 p.m. or so. Buy Pedialyte. Delete the sobriety counter from my phone. Buy Alka Seltzer. Sweat in the steam room at the Y. Drink just a single pint plus a few shooters. Go to a different liquor store because I don't like that the guy just hands me pints of Smirnoff at this point. In 4th grade I learned how fast a space shuttle flies. Kids would ask me to say it out loud because they thought it meant I was smart. I told them each time, though after a while they must have known it for themselves.

All night it was Alka Selzter and Tums and Omeprazole and Pedialyte. Maybe I can pull out on Day 4. Usually not, but let's say this time I do. Only 16 drinks yesterday so aside from some light pancreatitis I'm good. I manage to make it out of the day without drinking by binge eating instead. One of the solutions to the Fermi Paradox is that anyone we could have talked to is already dead. The universe used to be much warmer. We are a winter people.

Day 5: Wake up clear-ish with just some wrecked guts to deal with. Diarrhea and indigestion and the long tail of over the counter sleeping pills. Track down and throw away the various packs of cigarettes I bought over the last few days. Search through my Facebook messages and am relieved that I only hit on a few women, none of whom I know very well. It could be wishful thinking but they didn't seem to be offended by it. Spend day hydrating and taking antacids and painkillers. The treadmill was invented in the 19th century as a way to punish and reform prisoners. It's not the drinking I'm in love with. It's the getting better.

She asked me again, if anything I said was true, if I hated her, if I loved her like I said I did, so many times, drunk. And the best I could manage is: I thought they were true when I said them, or yes I meant them, or sometimes they were true. It's an interesting question. Truth. If it exists, if I ever had it from the beginning. If she should have known better than to have an affair with someone who has taken several graduate-level English courses on postmodernism and even did most of the reading. I don't know if they were true, Nikki, but I have a theory.

Salt and snow preserve South Bend through the worst of winter's months. Look at Lincolnway West. How else could so many signs stand witness for the failed restaurants and shuttered churches, the convenience stores of long, long ago? The snow and salt are a preservative of thankful funding. We can't forget that a grocery used to be in that building beside the scrapyard. We can't lose track of the sales of Memorial days past, of what our mothers remembered.

IV

Elise Cowen is on her way to die. A shimmering flock of glass travels with her. She leaves behind the seventh floor apartment of her parents and a scattering of poems that will find their way into print thanks to memory and how it finds it level like water. Elise Cowen, once she lands, will he remembered for once dating Allen Ginsberg. In a photo she walks slightly behind him, her hair cropped short. New York in winter. They carry themselves like youth who have meaning to make. Elise's doctors will remember her for her fits of psychosis and depression. But right now Elise is as the breaking wave or the pour. The water is free in the instant between the pitcher and the vase.

Ralph Cheever Dunning, meanwhile, will be remembered because Hemingway said he threw a very good bottle for a poet. While Elise Cowen arcs high overhead in a different decade Ralph lays dying, emaciated, in a filthy Parisian apartment. It is 1930. He dies like a child of the age. The 20s catch our hearts like Paris does. Ralph knew Ezra Pound and published poems about birds who cannot see him for he is dead and drowned. In his last days he sometimes walks to the window on skeletal feet and scrapes at the frost on the window with long fingernails until he can see some of Paris beyond. The lights yellow and warm. Although Ezra gives him opium he trades it for pigeons, which he sets free with poems tied to their legs. Incredibly, all of them will come home just in time to say goodbye. Their wings will cover him as he shivers and they will coo sweet, secret songs when he starts to cry.

I want to be able to speak to myself in a language of my choosing. I want that language to give flesh to things otherwise unutterable. The Germans have a word for checking your messages after drinking and hoping you didn't do anything stupid. The French have a word for getting into an argument and coming up with a real zinger of a comeback on the way home. I am the iPhone on which God is tweeting out his message and I blame autocorrect for any real mistakes I've made along the way.

Rozz Williams has hanged himself. It has been several minutes and he still sways as a pendulum. He has left a rose and a tarot card on the table. The tarot card is the Hanged Man. Rozz Williams has made art. Earlier he watched the movie Isadora and told his friend, who left halfway through, "Wait, you don't know how it ends!" How could he pass up an opening like that? Sometimes the ending to the movie just seems to write itself.

The 20s are nearly over. You can see it. From the top of the steps at *Sacre Coeur* the lights blink out singly while to the East threateningly dark storm clouds seem to gather. You can see them at sundown while drunk on cheap wine. Jacques Rigaut knows this. He's just visited Cheever and assured him the exit is soon. The pigeons were breathing in unison. So were the candles. Back home, Jacques carefully arranges things. It is November 1929 and too damned late. He fits his bed with a rubber sheet and measures the distance to his heart with a ruler. This is not suicide. This is giving everything for art. The bullet that drives into his heart will release all of the blood in the world to save the shattered and stumbling. Save them from the years that watch them with fangs bared. That watch them from the shadows as they walk through the woods, their lanterns small and flickering.

It is December of 1929. New York. I imagine the air thick with champagne corks. Jazz in Harlem. Okay. This is best I can do. Harry Crosby is sitting in a Manhattan apartment. He is ready to kill something beautiful so it does not grow old. He is doing this for us. So we will not grow old, either. Music drifts up to the window from a phonograph in a café. The clarinet tones beat themselves against the falling snow as they rise. The air suddenly becomes a flock of pigeons that merge with the smoke from the brownstone rooftops. Harry checks the mirror to make sure the world is watching. I am. We are. His true love waits for him on the bed with a heart that beats like a countdown. She raises her eyes to him as he crosses the floor to the bed. We can't wait any longer. Poetry is a gun.

It is 2003 and Reetika Vazirani is surprised how easily a butcher's knife passes through the flesh of her two-year-old son's arm. It is 1966 and a skinny young man named Yusuf sweats through his army greens in Vietnam. Meanwhile, Reetika is four. She watches a cow in the street lazily nose through a pile of rubbish. It is 1993 and Yusuf wins the Pulitzer Prize. It is 2001 and his semen finds purchase in Reetika's welcoming womb. It is 1995 and Reetika receives substantial praise for her debut book of poetry *White Elephants*. It is 2003 again. Reetika lays herself out beside her son and buries a new knife into her own arm, her flesh screaming for something that feels like a mother losing a son.

What do you see that separates a book from the distant, echoing scream of a cat some alleyways distant? *The Wind in the Willows* is the difference. Toad and Badger are the duality of the 20th Century man. As Jacques Rigaut lays himself out on his bed, holding a pistol to his heart, Mr. Toad waits in the street below, happily listening to the *put put put* of his motorcar engine. As Jacques pulls the trigger the air fills with will o' the wisp that spills from the apartment and down the stairs and into the street like glowing tufts of milkweed. Watch to see who follows them down to that black pavement. It is the moment a chorus of cats begin to remember the stories they scream into the night.

To cope with a life imprisoned we must either become institutionalized or become escape artists. Often, only the woman herself will know which she chose and sometimes not even then. To the outsider (to everyone) some patterns may seem apparent but translation is at best a blind, drunken lurch through the dark. Theresa Wilms-Mott escaped from a convent when she was 23. First to Chile, then Europe. On her last night in Paris it was close to Christmas. She noticed a strange young man staring mournfully at the entrance to the Gare du Nord and crying. She walked up asked him. He said his problem was a world without end. As she walked back to the hotel it looked at the same time like a wall and a tunnel.

Please cover this page in arrows drawn in red ink. Pointing in or out or around. That's up to you. Draw by feeling. I'm curious to see where you think my words point to. This used to be common. That's why you scarcely see a book of poems from the 1800s without at least half of the pages covered in bright red arrows. People thought it gave ghosts a visual guide to ethereal meaning. An unmarked book was an unread book, or a book read by a bad reader. Draw now. Point to the places where you love me.

I imagine that if I placed this manuscript into a lidless blender in a rented beach house that the letters would fly out through windows and ride strange air currents like milkweed seeds and grow into a thousand trees bearing fruit. I imagine that the fruit will remind anyone who eats it of how it feels to find romance in a poster of New York City at night, wondering who was in the still-lit windows and not thinking that they're probably just janitors or working late. The truth of it is we're building fucking concentration camps. Right now. We're putting children in them. I'll leave some room here. Please tell me everything turned out okay.

This is where you can tell me that everything turned out okay:

_____
_____
_____
_____
_____
_____
_____
_____
_____

Generally, I experience two types of memories: numbered memories and lettered memories. This is not as intuitive as one might assume. The first fuck is a lettered memory when many argue it should be numbered. Numbered memories include tattoos, the silence of fog, and the camaraderie of snow. Lettered memories are sometimes dangerous. This is because letters can't be added. Language lacks the elegance of math. You may think they are numbered right up until the moment you misspell some desperate devotional. The Aboriginal Australians classified fireflies in the same category as thorns. I can't speak for them, but I wonder if it was a way to avoid such unnecessary spelling errors.

I think the lesser of two destructions must be forgiven by the greater. It must be. It has to be. My sponsor told me that smoking was okay. As long as I'm sober, I can smoke. I smoke while I drink, too, but then nothing is okay. This is true of many worlds. If a poet means one thing she must write something that means two things. When my mother stopped leaving the house altogether she moved through the stacks of newspapers and boxes like a heavy, drunken ghost. Kept because in that complex sedimentary geology the world can write its own histories. It took us weeks to explore the ruins. As long as I don't love a thing too much I can make amends to the rest.

Dig into paper; these secrets. Not the words or the writing. Or even what is between them. It's best if they aren't opened at all. Childhood and salt. Childhood and forgetting. Jim built a library for Pam. The library collected things as they collected things and eventually we could not walk through it and instead scaled the uncertain landscape of plastic totes and overloaded, pregnant boxes. After Pam was left alone the box canyons grew until they snaked through the house. She collected anything printed. Newspapers, magazines, free weekly supermarket mailers. How could I have excavated such a thing properly? I had no training. How lucky I am that this vastness remained long after we swept. That's done. The emptied library now absent of dust and oddities. The books belong to other houses, if they belong to anyone, if they didn't find their way to the landfill. Pam stopped obsessively re-reading a biography of Stanford White, stopped passing out so it would fall out of her lap. Books no longer came home by boxful from the public library sale, unread for decades, bought because they were old and therefore precious and needed to be kept safe and unopened.

I watched a man in Egypt patiently working a bronze plate with a hammer and chisel. It was exquisitely etched with interlocking geometric patterns. The shop was a stop on a bus tour of several archaeological sites the names of which I do not recall. Halfway through a cruise down the Nile. My dad amused himself by handing out money to a crowd of children by the cafe. I took photos of the man working the bronze plate. A woman from New Zealand complained that the beggars ruined all of the stops. Father paid $40 for one of the handmade plates. I didn't tell him that the man never actually touched the chisel to the plate. Or that, as we were pulling away, I saw the man pick up one of the children to whom my father had given money. Or how the man tossed him high into the air, or how the boy laughed.

The strangest battle of World War 2 happened on May 5, 1945. American soldiers fighting alongside German army defectors defended Castle Itter in Austria against a group of Waffen SS. It was the only battle in which Americans and Germans fought on the same side. The defenders included a French tennis star and a former French Prime Minister. As things draw to a close we never know quite what to do with ourselves. Atmospheres feel strange. Endings can be elusive. The strangest battle of World War 2 happened three days before the war ended. The next day an American private named Joseph walked through the castle with a sense of urgency in his chest. He tried to find a place to look out the window at Europe. Some place poignant, where he could watch the world change. Later, he had sex with Andreas, a lovely boy from Munich who had only joined the Wermacht three months earlier. They both came. As Joseph licked the last drops of cum from Andreas' cock he could feel the world shifting. In Berlin, five hundred miles to the north, café proprietor picked through the rubble of houses looking for any surviving fine China. As he turned over a cup he found it was full of tiny seashells.

V

It is closing in on Trotsky's last few weeks in Mexico City. He is on the balcony, smoking and fiddling with the knob of a Bakelite radio until he finds something jazzy and French. A breeze breaks the hot, heavy night air and Trotsky sees the tops of buildings begin to blow into the air like ripe, white dandelions. Frieda Kahlo and Diego Rivera start a lazy, swaying dance in the next room. Her arm hangs to her side holding a gin that splashes onto the carpet. In the street below several men sweat and play backgammon and sip Coca Cola. Trotsky wears his exile like a finely tailored suit. He meets important people. He reminds the world he is still here. Cats gather on a fence and sing to him in a Greek chorus. Somewhere in the city an ice pick waits, mundane and not yet famous.

Some of the ancient Greek statues at the Art Institute of Chicago just aren't very good, even allowing for time and erosion and the work of history. One carved head in particular struck me as notably amateurish. I wonder if the artist would be embarrassed to see it on display now. If she went on to carve much more beautiful things and if this gape-eyed, rough-hewn head was just an early exercise in learning the human form. If she'd say, "God, I can't believe that thing survived. I threw it in a fucking lake."

The Neanderthals were unquestioned masters of the world for two. Hundred. Millennia. Smoke, the spirit of forest. It took us what, a few hundred years after the industrial revolution to really fuck up the place? After college I spent some time drunk and sad in Paris. My friend Lee taught me how to use a screwdriver and a hammer to open a bottle of wine, pushing the cork into the bottle like an argument. And how to roll cigarettes with salvaged tobacco from butts in ashtrays, complete with a re-used filter because we waste nothing. We use every part of this modern life.

Wine is not the spirit of the French. That is a folk tale. Geneticists will tell you it is paint and not just because it fueled the Salon. The subject holds all the power. Never the painter. The male gaze is an empty, brittle thing. Look at Suzone in the *Folies-Bergère*. Her expression is familiar to all women who have had to carry on awful conversations with creeps while bartending. Creeps who call themselves artists or nice guys. Manet painted her with oranges, meaning she was a prostitute. But she wasn't. She already had his money. And the mirror? Go back and look at the painting. She's still there. And the oranges are just some ripe and lovely fruit.

In the photo Luca is squatting. Von Gloeden usually posed his models with props evoking ancient Greek myth but Luca will have none of that. His penis is as dark as the skin on his arms. He props his face on his hands. Elbows on his knees. As the shutter clicks, the sun in Southern Italy is perfect and pregnant. At night Luca sometimes goes down to the sea and masturbates into the ocean. The lights on the hills opposite sing back to him with his own name. Salt and the days. He stiffens when the German photographer's finger writes its way down his stomach. Some of the dust that blows in through the window when he poses was once part of the Sahara and crossed a sea to get to him. Proof that old and young things both can be so beautiful in the hands of the right artist.

Everyone seems to be wrong about moonlight. Well, almost everyone. A few got it right. The Sami believed in silence at the Solstice. The Igbo that Ala carried dead ancestors in her womb. And the Etruscans knew that Losna controlled the tides. There is a photo called "The Pond — Moonlight" by Edward Steichen. It is an early color photo, made in 1904. The moon shines through a stand of trees beside a still pond in rural New York. Edward sensed that taking a photo of the moon could turn the world into a flat disc. In the pond you can see past the moon. Just over one hundred miles, where Ezra Pound is writing a poem for Hilda Doolittle. A movement starts to settle over the Earth. Lazily at first. It will take them all to such different places, even though they are so young. Edward taps you on the shoulder now, before you get too lost beyond the trees, and points skyward. The stars move in dense rivers like a Van Gogh. The universe gives form to itself through its own voice.

Of course some people still debate the true nature of *erastes* and *eromenos*. Words mean different things at different times, different languages. For us it's the sex. Most sex was probably intercural, although at least one vase depicts an *eromenos* about climb onto the lap of his *erastes,* who is fully erect. Of course the *erastes* also shared poetry and philosophy and love with his eromenos. The Romans kept the sex and weren't as interested in all that mentorship stuff. A bunch of fuckboys in togas. This was a poverty for the eromenos. We might have lost it altogether if not for the Romantic poets. Because the point was: something beautiful to breathe. When Byron saw the water coursing down John Edleston's slim, pale body he believed that what Vitruvius wrote about beauty must be true. Believed it in a way without speaking. I felt that once, but with a coyote of all things. It appeared out of an alleyway in a Chicago snowstorm at night. Padded out from behind a dumpster and froze as it saw me. In the best of all worlds it would have spoken or given me a quest but instead it trotted off into that bright, orange air until I couldn't see it anymore.

In 1816 a doctor named René Laennec invented the stethoscope because he was uncomfortable with pressing his ear to a woman's breast to hear her heart. The first model was a simple wooden tube with a fitting on the end for the ear and within a decade the stethoscope had acquired a more familiar form. Today, millions of doctors around the world use Dr. Laennec's invention. Around the same time, doctors began massaging women's genitals with vegetable oil to induce a state of paroxysm and relieve hysteria. The problem was the labor intensive nature of the treatment. The invention of electricity solved that. An English doctor named Joseph Mortimer Granville invented the electrical percusser, a vibrating wand which allowed women to induce their own paroxycal states at home. As medical science ceased to recognize hysteria as a medical disorder and instead as simple functioning sexuality the electrical percusser fell almost entirely out use. Today they're remembered as a medical curiosity, popular only among collectors of the strange and macabre, a great addition to any curio cabinet.

Lena Kochman believed she was being followed by the United States Postal Service. Go Google her. There are compilation videos. She filmed herself confronting postal workers on the street and telling them to stop stalking her. She made blogs about this. Articulated the connections. She saw an ad for curtains in a magazine and then she saw an ad on a bench for a Dr. Curtin. She thought that when men touched their noses around her it meant they thought she had a smelly vagina. She thought something called The Conglomerate was behind all of this. Lena made these videos and posts while living in a women's shelter in Boston and using public library computers. Her videos were popular on the Public Freakouts subreddit. She did this for years but she hasn't posted anything in a long while now. Nobody was listening. The postmen kept coming.

More than anything I associate the 90s with a mighty struggle to break free of the tyranny of fonts. This is probably because I was young for much of them yet I remember all of them, and the 90s were mostly a marketing scheme. But if my associations are correct it must because Basquiat would paint in expensive Armani suits. He would walk around in the same, splattered with paint. Hear me out when I say that Basquiat's painting "Skull" predicted the shaking, wacky fonts of early 90s Nickelodeon. Eventually they buy everything. And they buy it wrong. Basquiat painted the sound of a skull screaming at itself. They always buy it wrong. When white people started playing the blues they couldn't have known what it really meant.

I tried and failed to achieve erection in that bed in Beirut. How perfect the setting. The windows open and the call to prayer rising nearby and the sunset over the Mediterranean visible through blowing white curtains. Wine drunk and a woman there. A writer, more. A goddamned foreign correspondent. She skirted from room to room, nude, and we smoked on her balcony. Yet, nothing. I never made travel last. I left France after only a few months without writing a word. She told me about accidentally driving through ISIS held villages and I hated to hear her tell it. Me, soon to fly home to Indiana. I tried to make it okay by going down on her for a long, long time. I've always been a tourist.

My friend's dad decorated his basement according to a Jimmy Buffet theme. A sign said "The weather is here, wish you were beautiful." What is it about Jimmy Buffet that suddenly entrances middle-aged white men precisely at the point where they should never again be shirtless at a beach? I have not visited many beaches. I can produce a curated list of women I've slept with that reads like footnotes in the poet's biography. When I was engaged or married, no matter. Sarah, the poet in the park by Shakespeare and Company, when I was still so sad. Francine, the English Major from my modernism class. Deborah, the sad girl with cuts on her arms in Edinburgh. Maria, tender and sensitive, cheating in grad school. Patty in my car in the rural Illinois dark, hurried and secret. Or, later, in the tall grass near an abandoned farmhouse. I used to hope this is what poets do, and not just for the sake of their biographies. Because they just feel so much more. Because they had to write about something doomed before the beach called them home. It's nice to think that bullshit, even now.

My mother drew "danger dots" on things to remind us to be safe. She usually used post-it notes but if the thing was particularly dangerous she bypassed the post-it and used a red sharpie. The stove, for example. Bright red danger dots by the burner knobs to remind us to turn them off. A danger dot on the drawer that held the knives to remind us that there were knives inside. She broke the long handles off of pots so we wouldn't accidentally knock them off. A few years ago I was boiling water and my hip brushed against a pot handle and almost knocked it off of the stove onto my dog, who was waiting patiently for me to drop a piece of whatever I was cooking. She was right about the pot handles. She never placed any warnings on the half-gallon bottles of vodka that killed her. But then, mothers need to leave some sort of mystery behind. Mystery is the gift. Inheritance is a shit jackpot. We still count our winnings.

VI

The stubby, jagged rows of cornstalks through the snow reminded me of teeth or desperate finger bones. Illinois, clawing its way toward the sun.

I remember when dogs took you like water. Could take anyone. Left a vapor trail of you, an avatar of dust, standing until the wind got there. It's like you had love as coins. That's love with end. If a heart could fashion as a bow, teeth as a barrette. You asked me to crawl into you in places. The ones that needed someone else's flesh. But the side-eye dog said not to trust anyone who just leaves his bones laying around like that.

On place names: San Jose, Illinois, twenty miles east of Havana, the Illinois River town. Pronounced "San-Joze," with a hard J. Population 642. Versailles, Illinois, an hour's drive downriver. The locals pronounce it "Ver-saylz." Population 478. Fifty miles south of Havana, and two miles from one another, Berlin and New Berlin, Illinois. Both pronounced with the emphasis on the "Ber," not the "lin." Population and 130 and 1,030, respectively. An hour west of Havana, a creek called Drowning Fork. Pronounced like you think. Named because two soldiers are said to have drowned attempting to cross it in 1827. Drowning Fork is too narrow, too shallow a little thing to be named in such a way. Scarcely 10 miles long. I've jumped it. Literally jumped it. Drowning Fork empties into the La Moine, which empties into the Illinois, which empties into Mississippi which joins the Ohio River at Cairo, Illinois. Pronounced "Cay-row." Population 2,800.

On November 11, 1909, around ten thousand people gathered in Cairo, Illinois, to watch the lynching of William "Froggie" James, a black farm laborer accused without evidence of murdering a young white shop clerk named Mary Pelly. In the photo the crowd is so thick the camera cannot reach the edges. Two men have shimmied up a light pole for a better view. Over the crowd two great arches of electric lights drench the attendees in the warm, yellow embrace of the 20th century. The next morning city waste workers were tasked with cleaning up the square. Given that the lynching was a spontaneous affair, no thought had been given to additional public waste bins. They're still cleaning it up. It's become a generational effort. Like a company town built around a coal mine, or the city of skilled artisans who built the Great Pyramid of Giza, handing off the labor from father to son and so on.

At Dickson Mounds near Lewistown, Illinois, the Dickson family used the contents of 800 graves as foundation fill for a new farmhouse. We took field trips there to look at the skeletons of the people they didn't destroy. The archaeologists carefully excavated the graves and put them on display. Whole families. Mothers with infants. The infant skeletons were my favorite. I remember people were so angry when they finally covered the burial following years of Native protests. The skeletons were the highlight of the tour, they said, and without them it was just another boring museum. We didn't go on another field trip there after they covered them. The next year we went to the ag-mech show and I got to stick my hand through a fistula opened to allow access into a cow's stomach, to feel whatever it was digesting, and they assured me that the cow didn't mind at all.

I had to get some gas before your funeral, not that I really felt so enthusiastic about gas I just needed it and wouldn't you know it, cigarettes and coffee and all the things people buy? Yes I saw people buying them in front of me and I thought it felt so weird that people still need cigarettes and coffee when you die and weird too that their money would even work, right? There cannot be one reason, one goddamned reason why that should be the case, but speaking about it now I have to remind myself it's not like you weren't so terribly important and alive.

I told her the socks at a gas station are really for huffing paint when she bought socks at a gas station. The socks are for huffing paint, shoelaces are for shooting junk, the Chore-Boy scouring pads and those little plastic roses are for smoking crack and she said, *Oh, I was going to use them on my feet.*

At the dollar store I saw a woman return to her husband holding a gallon jug of tea and say, I found this tea for a dollar and he said, that looks good that will be nice to have later on the deck. I thought, how can this not be a land of plenty and promise when you can have a nice thing later for only a dollar?

Sometimes I get on Google street view and look at places I used to live, hoping to catch a glimpse of myself or my ex-wife or our car or anything that proves I was that person, before I wasn't, before I became this one and all of the many I have been in between. Hoping there really is something approaching a narrative. I've never succeeded, though once using satellite view I did see what might have been my 2006 Oldsmobile Alero parked at my ex-wife's parents' house in Cary. When I drive through the towns in Western Illinois it seems like they crash landed there. Not that they were once founded and prosperous and their people grew grain, corn, hogs and wool. That the survivors crawled out of the wreckage of an ill-fated generational spaceship and built what they could out of scavenged scrap.

And he said don't seek your fortune in business, and you didn't and she said don't just do what will make you happy but you were happy when you did and he said be the change you want to see or something and no one has time for that and she said go west young man and you did that once and they all said better the devil you know and she was and someone sang that you should never trust a poet, and we all saw how well that worked out for you and you said Oh God! and God said a whole bunch of shit and all I'm saying is brother can you spare a dime?

Once, I lead a girl on a scavenger hunt. Once, I moved across the world for a girl. Once, I was always drunk and read all of Emily's poems and thought I loved Emily, too. Do these things while you're young. Only youth gives meaning to gesture. Remember how light it felt: feathers, hollow bones, paper towels and how gently you placed it in the earth. How many mark these maps?

Christmas in the Northwest Suburbs. It's 2009 and I'm feeling hopeful with the recent election and with leaving in a few days to move to Bloomington, Indiana. I'm in Cary, at my now-ex-wife's parents. Her father is very drunk. He keeps running to the garage to fiddle with decorations and when he comes back he is glassy eyed and content. I used to hide bottles in the ceiling of the basement so I could drink while I did laundry. I did a lot of laundry. He is passionate about Christmas decorations. It is also Christmas in New York and Rachel Wetzsteon is 42. I don't think she knows it but she's just about right on the mark. The Wikipedia category, "Poets who committed suicide" contains 152 entries. The average age of a poet suicide is 42 years, six months. I did the math. Rachel wrote that in a leaf scatter she saw versions of herself she was on the verge of becoming. Winter is a leaf-less time. An infinite future, then. The Grubbes of Cary, Illinois preferred artificial trees. I remember how their dog Fonzi always came to my lap and how, with a deep sigh, he'd sink into me while I sat on the floor and we'd watch all the comings and goings of the holidays.

I wonder if any of the kids from Arcade Fire songs ever visited any convenience store parking lot from a Modest Mouse song. Did they fall in love over 90s top 40 radio there? Grow up and move back to the suburbs to take their turn? Are they strangers, even to themselves?

VII

Is it true? At the end of this am I wrapping myself in a small South Bend life, cocooned as if in spider web? It's not nothing, nor is it needful. Parties were always the worst unless I was drunk, anyway. I don't believe I could have lived in New York without the ready comfort of a half-pint in my hip pocket. As at the party so it is that I stay out of the way in my own overgrown backyard. I cannot use the burn pit for the family of groundhogs who have crafted a burrow beneath the ring rock. I try not to use the garage because I don't like to scare the few feral cats living there, who watch from a distance as I put out food, who move through the alleys like a rumor. In summer I often cannot open the back door because the corbels and the door jamb make an ideal fitting for spider webs. I fear I would move through any other life in a series of long orbits around familiar liquor stores. It's hard enough to stay sober here, and none of the friends in my yard even ask me to make small talk at their parties.

It's cool enough to sleep with windows open. Enjoy the trains that remind me of Bushnell and listen: a strange mass migration of dogs has begun. Every night they pad east by the hundreds along the tracks toward Elkhart. Heading, no doubt, for the switching yard, to meet others coming in from much stranger places than South Bend. I think the dogs will find a black ring of trees around several acres of concrete, the site of a lost factory in southern Ohio. One of the sites that several explorers from the Royal Geographic Society have already vanished while trying to find. The dogs will form a series of concentric rings and stare due north waiting for the stars to shift. Their chorus of yips and barks and howls is a blast of horns announcing the return of some lost, violent century. Looking now, I can see them trotting along the tracks. Singly their silhouettes pass in front of a light in the parking lot of a motorcycle dealership. Wait: I think they may be spelling out a message in Morse code.

The ancient MFA programs taught that poetry was an act of devotional translation or, sometimes, codebreaking. All codes led to the Muse. Thanks to the Historical Arts we know this isn't entirely true. The Empire of Urartu was forgotten until the 19th century. In 1827 a German explorer discovered a large tablet of Urartian history but was killed by bandits before he could translate it. The same thing happened a few years later to a German archaeologist. In 1840, a British expedition reached the tablet but fled a bandit attack and barely escaped with their lives. Exactly 100 years later two Americans copied the tablet but their notes were lost when their ship, the Athenia, was torpedoed and sunk by a U-boat under the command of Captain Fritz Lemp. A year later Captain Lemp's submarine was captured along with an Enigma machine, finally allowing the codebreakers at Bletchley Park to unravel German secrets and win the war. Lemp drowned trying to return to the ship and sink it and the world became a little less mysterious.

Isaac Newton was 23 when the plague closed Trinity College and sent him home from his studies for a semester of sick days. Bored as hell, he played with prisms, splitting light into rainbows. Here's the thing, though. No one thought that the spectrum was actually in the light. They thought the prism just colored light as a trick. Newton had the idea of the second prism. Held up to the blue portion, it added no more colors. Light was not white. The color was in the light itself. Van Gogh was 36 when madness sent him into the asylum at Saint-Paul-de-Mausole lunatic asylum for a year of hydrotherapy and walks. One night he held his canvas up to the stars over Saint-Rémy-de-Provence. A prism can return a fractured spectrum to the whole. Algebra in light. When Van Gogh opened himself with a bullet all of the yellow light in the universe spilled from the wound. Famously, it was so bright that some of the townsfolk thought it was morning and started their day several hours early.

Audubon noted that migrations draw sound from the world like a needle on a record. Not that the cries of geese or a million-strong hoof print stampede is music. Far from it. Both are absent of rhythm. And so with the desperate flights of entire families north through Mexico or across the Mediterranean on oft-doomed little ships. What he meant is, one might consider that the first record-ed human voice was a song about a person who begs for a quill to write because his candle is dead, because there is no more light, for the love of God.

Because I must write about Illinois or else Illinois will cease to ease itself sensuously along the riverbank, like a lover lounging on an old cast-iron bed, sighted through heirloom lace curtains that blow in and an out of a peeling window frame in a McDonough County farmhouse. Illinois leans into Iowa. Iowa can feel hot breath on its neck. The smell of whiskey and smoke. Iowa feels itself stiffen in the thrill of it all. Illinois presents itself in an act of sheer audacity. Iowa whispers, "what if people see?"

As a child I took Tae Kwon Do in a strip mall parking lot. A dojo sandwiched between a pizza place and a pawn shop. On the wall: a poster:

"Enough pails of water, a river. Enough shovels of earth, a mountain" - Ancient Chinese Proverb.

I have been unable to determine the authenticity of the proverb, but when I was in grade school we took a field trip to Cahokia Mounds. Monks Mound is the largest earthen pyramid in the world. A millennium ago a Mississippian people piled 22 million baskets of earth at Cahokia. Europeans did not believe that Natives could have built these things and invented the Mound Builder Myth, a lost European race, to explain the achievements. Either that or ignored them outright. Now we don't deny the origin of the mounds. Now we give graduate assistantships to gifted young students who want to learn about them. When I was a child I wanted to be an archaeologist when I grew up. I've often regretted quitting Tae Kwon Do after testing for my red belt.

Repetition gives meaning to music. We call that rhythm. I learned about a cockatoo that understands rhythm but not melody. Melody is still the domain of humanity. Repetition makes prayer of earnest desire. Repetition of prayer is a path to God. I want the world to turn around me like a prayer wheel, this world that does not see us hold our faces to the sky and wait for God to take a picture from the angle that makes us look our thinnest. And I want to the world to preserve you in colors and in vibrato, in skies of yellow. Years on it's like I'm looking at you through honey. Repetition is the vibration that gives form to aether. Repetition can make us come. Repetition cuts a desire path across the university commons, diminishes returns on I Love You, and shortens days just when we need them to be longer again.

You've thought of this before, that a river cannot belong to a city. A lake, sure, but a river? A river moves. The water is only through the city in transit. What the city really owns is the bit of channel that funnels the water on closer to the sea or the lake that will claim it. It would seem strange to call Pittsburgh a channel town, so we stick with the river, while we can see it. Start there, then. In Pittsburgh. City of Bridges. Steel City. City of Champions. City Where You've Never Slept. Pittsburgh where I think you watched me ride sodium-yellow fog as if crowd-surfing, out from the shore of the river into an arch-backed landscape. I think if you followed me then your eyes were fixed on a single star point. They nailed me to a tree branch in coal country. They stripped me over. They threw me into the river to meet you again, years later, when I finally join the Father of Waters near Cairo.

It's tempting to write, if you've lived at the coast, that the Earth-long persistent thrum of the surf is the heartbeat of the sea. Or maybe the breath. And fun to write that after four billion years the ocean is bored in such a profound way that the word needed to express such boredom cannot be uttered in a single human lifetime. And the surf is ticking off tally marks on a prison wall. But today I learned that a team of mathematicians has calculated Pi out to 31.4 trillion digits. I didn't know they were still figuring this number, this endless number. I really hope they find something soon.

The crows have opened a recycling plant behind my house. They start work early and I can't sleep in anymore. They stopped bringing me random bits of aluminum. Now they bring me rent instead. This is less romantic, but they've done a great job of cleaning up the neighborhood. I used to talk a lot about the intelligence of crows, but I never gave any real thought as to their entrepreneurial spirit.

What if fire remembers that we were all birthed from it? What if fire hates showing up unannounced but burns all of the letters it tries to send? In January, fire sits with fire at a bar in South Bend called the Mannerchor Club. Bottles burst behind the bar and fire is thirsty. Fire pours itself a double. Fire asks if it was ever in New York. Yes, fire replies. Fire loved a girl named Yetta. Fire watched her from the lamp wick as she bathed, from her father's match, from the gaslight as she walked home from the shirtwaist factory. One day fire had to meet her. Fire still remembers how she moved through fire's embrace. How her body met fire like a mountain meets the sunset. How fire followed her out the window into the street below, singing a devotional so sweet that no human song could give it voice.

I came to understand that poetry is a craft, like building a cabinet or laying brick. The better I understood this the more I yearned for the ready give of wood and stone. Something to cut and bruise my flesh. To imprint upon me evidence of my own work ethic. Not that the work is easier. More, that the wood cannot refuse its transformation. How frustrating, then, that, having abandoned the keyboard for the woodshop, I find myself screaming at a pile of lumber which stubbornly refuses to turn itself into a chair.

Sarah takes shorts on a cigarette, standing in salt and snow, on the shiny, dark sidewalk beside McCormick's in downtown South Bend. The last few puffs, looking at the vault of downtown, garish red lips sucking the already wet filter, itself bummed and kept behind the ear of the fattening boy who enrolled at Notre Dame three years ago and took a semester off a year later and made his way tonight through this darkened dive, gliding side and front like the sudden flow of a bird flock to find the fucked up girl at the pool table who shaved her head last night, drunk and crying and cutting, who drained her beer and gave him a kiss and a smoke from the pack she stole from her work at the discount tobacco shop and when she arrived at the bar tonight it was to high fives, hugs, inside jokes with the door man and everyone knows her and sometimes she feels it's like a family here, and warm.

How to find me: Tear out the first page of this book. Write what you need. Tuck it into a collection of Hart Crane or Sylvia Plath. Toss the book into the St. Joe River, downtown, above the dam. As it sinks to the bottom, a young, precocious catfish will be nibbling on the toes of a drowned man who fell into the river late last year in Elkhart. He has been making his way to the end, to the beach in Michigan where he remembered riding the carousel, running through the dunes, the first time he cupped a breast in his hand, sitting by the lighthouse on that perfect August night. The ghost of the man will wonder what has caught the attention of the fish and will read your note before setting off on a slow, quiet quest to deliver it to me. I promise.

Feeling well in South Bend as in: summer and feeling the rest of the city through the low gone light. As in the light that throws the rest of the summer into sharp relief. I stop at the bookshop on Michigan Street. I see the half-empty pint glasses on the patio picnic tables at the brew pub underneath the old State Theatre Marquis. God, this weather, this energy, suddenly this joy. They seem so happy. Five attractive people drinking together. I buy no books at the bookstore and I'm thinking about that first beer, that first cigarette, about a friend who arrives and we are all so happy to see each other. I go alone to the dam by the Century Center and smoke while watching a basketball continually get sucked under and pop back up after several agonizing seconds. I find myself in silent cheer every time it resurfaces. Certain names live on my tongue as an act of devotion. Diane Arbus, Joe Bolton. *Generación decapitada*. John Allyn Smith swims through eddies on his back and spits water into the air. A sea of trees obeys the landscape like any other sea. I see diners at a waterside restaurant patio. Drinkers in sunglasses and polo shirts. Servers move quickly through this warmth, this giving, wonderful warmth, this pregnant afternoon, this nothing, this insulation.

The greatest thing I learned this year is that the Easter Island heads are actually entire statues buried up to their necks. They have arms, legs, bellybuttons. No, really. Look it up. And isn't that great? Everyone thought they were so mysterious, for so many years, these heads placed upright on the shore. We hadn't even broken the surface.

Acknowledgements

I would like to thank Louise Collins and David Dodd Lee, who were kind enough to read drafts of my work and share their wisdom with me. And I would especially like to thank Stephanie Erdman Forsythe for her work in reading multiple drafts and helping me arrange the poems into their present form. The narrative of this book, such as it is, would not exist without her. Finally, I would like to thank D.A. Lockhart for looking at a much disorganized, very early draft and seeing something in it that that warranted taking a chance and working with an author on his first collection.

About the Author

Craig Finlay is a transient. His poems are the works of a person who has traveled the world in search of himself and his place in it. He currently works as a librarian in rural southern Oklahoma, where he'll probably be for a little while until he moves somewhere else. His beard has its own bio and PO box.

9 781988 214375